A gift For:

....

From:

....

THE
DRUMMER
BOY

A Christmas Tale from
TED DEKKER

COUNTRYMAN

NASHVILLE, TENNESSEE

Like Daniel, may the truth of Christmas beat in your heart, embolden your spirit, and set you free to give your best to the King.

Once upon a time not so very far in the future, there lived a boy named Daniel. If Daniel was not the most famous boy who ever lived, he was certainly the bravest.

But Daniel wasn't always so brave. In fact, after the day he fell off his roof and broke both arms, he became one of the most cautious boys in the neighborhood.

His mother insisted that any child who'd fallen so far and been hurt so badly would certainly be as timid as Daniel. It was his good sense that made him careful.

Daniel was grateful for Mother's love, but no amount of motherly love helped him on the city streets, where all the other ten–year–olds were busy dodging honking cars and playing war behind large trash bins in the alleyways. He joined them on occasion. But he never liked the way they looked at his stiff white arms, his wrists frozen in place.

Daniel preferred to play Magnetix with his younger sister, Chelise, or better yet, watch his father playing the drums with the City Circus Orchestra.

The City Circus Orchestra. Now that was the real ticket. Daniel's one wish was to play the drums like Father played them, beating on the big bass, flipping his wrists on the snare, and thumbing the tall tom–toms. The mere idea of making such sounds in perfect rhythm kept him dreaming late into the night. But everyone knows that drummers need good wrists, and Daniel's wrists were as stiff as candy canes.

Daniel's impossible dream became a real hope

one day, December 18 to be precise, seven days before the Holiday.

Daniel sat cross-legged behind the balcony railing on the second floor of the Circus auditorium, watching the orchestra play their theme song as the audience filed out that chilly day. Elephants had stomped and tumblers had tumbled and the show was over. The lights would soon go out, and Father would pack away his drum until tomorrow when the show would start all over again.

Daniel watched Father proudly. He waved his right arm absentmindedly, mimicking the drumming motion. His arm moved well enough, but his wrist was useless. He'd beaten on a drum a thousand times and was always awkward.

A sound came out of the shadows. "Psst, boy." Mr. Pablo, the prop man, stood in the door that led into the upper hallway. Daniel liked the strange old man, but they didn't often speak.

"Come here, Danny boy." The thin, gray–haired man, who was a friend of his father, motioned to him. "Come, I have something to show you."

Daniel thought twice, then followed Mr. Pablo along the dim hall. The man ruffled Daniel's hair and smiled as they walked. "It's okay, boy. I think you'll like this."

He opened a door marked *Props: Keep Out.*

"I can't help noticing how much you like drums," Mr. Pablo said.

Daniel peered into the forbidden room. A shaft of sunshine spotlighted piles of colored balancing balls, juggling pins, nets, trapezes, and mats.

"Isn't that right?" Mr. Pablo said.

"Yes, sir. I do like drums."

"That's what I thought. Come in." The man peered back down the hall to make sure they weren't spotted. "Keep your voice down."

He closed the door and walked to a large trunk

in one corner. He bent to one knee, unlatched the lock, and opened the lid. Books and loose papers covered the bottom of the trunk, but Daniel caught his breath at the sight of a small, round drum on top.

"You like it?" Mr. Pablo asked, standing up.

"It's a drum. It's . . . it's beautiful!"

"Go on, pick it up."

Daniel lifted the small drum gingerly and held it in his stiff arms. The yellowed skin was smooth and taut. He'd seen pictures of drums like this, but he'd never actually touched one.

"It's not only beautiful," Mr. Pablo said, "it's special. Turn it over."

Daniel did so carefully. "Little Drummer Boy," he read aloud. "That's me?"

The prop man chuckled. "No, no, but I suppose it could be."

"Who was it?"

Mr. Pablo glanced at the door. "If I tell you

about this drum, it could be dangerous."

Daniel didn't care for danger, but he had to know. "Please tell me."

The man nodded and light sparkled in his eyes. "Have you ever heard of Christmas?"

"Christmas? What's Christmas?"

"Shh, shh." The man hushed Daniel with yet another glance at the door. "That's what the Holiday used to be called. But that name has been forbidden since before you were born."

"Christmas," Daniel whispered, casting a look at the door himself. "What's it mean?"

"Well, that's the secret, my boy. The Holiday wasn't always a time just for giving and getting presents. It once marked the birthday of a king named Jesus Christ." Mr. Pablo spoke the name so softly that Daniel could barely hear it.

"Jesus Christ?"

"Shhh…"

They stood in silence. "He was a king?" Daniel finally asked.

"Yes. And this drum was played for that very king by a boy known only as the Little Drummer Boy. People all over the world used to sing songs of Christmas and decorate their homes with scenes of King Jesus' birth and give gifts to celebrate his birthday."

Daniel looked at the drum with new respect and awe.

"Do you want the drum?" Mr. Pablo asked.

"Me? I can have it?"

The man smiled. "Consider it my Christmas gift to you."

"Really?"

"Really. It's yours."

DANIEL COULD HARDLY BELIEVE his good fortune. He was so delighted with his new drum that he rushed home, practically forgetting the story about the king.

"Mother, look!" he cried, rushing to the kitchen where the family was gathered for dinner. "Look at my drum."

Mother smiled wide. "Wow, such a beautiful drum. That's yours?"

Daniel told them about Mr. Pablo's gift to him.

"What a good idea," Father said. "I always liked Pablo. What a kind man. He said you could keep it?"

"Yes, he gave it to me. I think I could learn to play a drum this small, don't you think, Father?" Daniel set it down on the counter and awkwardly thumped the surface.

Father chuckled and graced them all with a perfectly executed roll on the old drum. "That's how you'll do it one day with enough practice, boy. It's a perfect gift."

"A perfect gift!" Chelise said. "My perfect gift would be a pony. Am I going to get a pony for the Holiday?"

"What, you think I own the whole City?" Father joked.

"Don't worry, Chelise, you can play my drum when I'm not," Daniel said.

They sat and ate Mother's meat loaf.

"Mr. Pablo said the drum was played for a king named Jesus Christ who was born on the Holiday. He said the Holiday used to be called Christmas."

Daniel's words silenced the clinking of his parents' forks. Father blinked and stared at Daniel.

"What are you saying? You can't say that, do you hear me? It's against the law."

"But at our table," Mother said. "Surely it won't do any harm . . ."

"I don't care. You will not utter such things at my table."

Daniel felt like he might cry. "But I . . ."

"But nothing, boy. We are employees of the City, and unless the Mayor himself moves heaven and earth to change the law, I will not allow those words to be spoken in my house."

"Who's Jesus Christ?" Chelise asked.

"Silence!" Father thundered.

Nothing else was said of the matter.

Daniel went to his room early, eager to spend time with his new drum. He examined it closely under the light, awed by the smooth hide and the soft leather strap and the pretty blue trim. What kind of boy had first owned this wonderful drum?

Daniel set the drum on his dresser across the room and watched it, imagining what it would be like to play it the next day. He soon fell asleep and dreamed.

Play for him, Daniel. Go on, play your drum for him.

He dreamed that he was standing over a cradle that held the baby king named Jesus. What a wonderful dream! He struck the drum, *pa rum pum pum pum.*

Sing for him, Daniel, the baby's mother said.

So he did. He played and he sang and the baby smiled.

Daniel awoke suddenly. He opened his eyes and stared into the dim light. He couldn't see the drum on the dresser because something—his pillow or one of his stuffed animals—sat right in front of his nose, blocking . . .

Daniel gasped and bolted up in bed. It was the drum! He glanced at the dresser. No drum. No drum there, because the drum was here, on his bed, right in front of him!

How was that possible? It wasn't!

He scrambled out of bed, turned on his light, and stared at the drum. Slowly he lifted it and examined it more closely.

It was then, while holding the instrument up to the bright light, that he saw the shadow of something inside the drum. He turned the drum every which way trying to figure out what it was.

Finally, too curious to ignore the mystery, he carefully untied the leather string that held the rims tight. It was hard going with his stiff wrists, but ten minutes later he lifted the skin.

Inside, a very old sheaf of papers had been taped to the wood. Daniel pried the papers loose, set the drum aside, and studied the black handwriting, his heart now hammering with the discovery.

The first page looked like a poem or song.

Little Drummer Boy

Come, they told me, pa rum pum pum pum
A newborn King to see, pa rum pum pum pum
Our finest gifts we bring, pa rum pum pum pum
To lay before the King, pa rum pum pum pum,
rum pum pum pum, rum pum pum pum,
So to honor Him, pa rum pum pum pum,
When we come.

Little Baby, pa rum pum pum pum
I am a poor boy too, pa rum pum pum pum

I have no gift to bring, pa rum pum pum pum
That's fit to give a King, pa rum pum pum pum,
rum pum pum pum, rum pum pum pum,
Shall I play for You, pa rum pum pum pum,
On my drum?

Mary nodded, pa rum pum pum pum
The ox and lamb kept time, pa rum pum pum pum
I played my drum for Him, pa rum pum pum pum
I played my best for Him, pa rum pum pum pum,
rum pum pum pum, rum pum pum pum,
Then He smiled at me, pa rum pum pum pum,
Me and my drum.

Daniel's hand began to tremble. A poor boy with a drum, just like in his dream! His eyes dropped to the bottom where someone had written something in blue ink:

I promise to keep the drum safe, Father, as you asked on your dying bed. It will one day again be played for the king.

Daniel swallowed. He was meant to find this drum. He turned to the second page. A story, it looked like. **The Birth and Life of Jesus Christ.**

Daniel read quickly. He read about the wise men who gave gifts to the baby king. He read about shepherds and about Mary and Joseph and about the temple. He read about the amazing things Jesus did when he grew up.

The more he read, the faster his little heart began to beat. This king named Jesus Christ had done many, many wonderful things. And perhaps the most wonderful thing he'd done, Daniel thought, rubbing his own stiff limbs, was to straighten the withered hand of a crippled man.

Tears welled in Daniel's eyes. Could there be such a king? Yes, there had to be! And maybe he'd been chosen to play the drum for the king. He'd dreamed about the song, and then the drum had floated across the room and landed by his head. It was impossible, but it had really happened.

And Holiday was really Christmas, the time of year when the whole world worshiped the king named Jesus and gave gifts to celebrate his birthday.

Daniel read the story again, walking as he read. Why hadn't Father or Mother told him about this king? Because it was unlawful. But why?

Father's anger drummed through his mind. *Unless the Mayor himself moves heaven and earth to change what is law. . .*

By the time Daniel hid the papers under his mattress, tied the skin tight, and turned off his light, he had made a decision. He was a cautious boy, but he could do what the Little Drummer Boy had done.

A shiver of fear slid through Daniel's bones. Could he really do it? Could such a small boy really play for the king?

Father had gone to the Circus to play and Mother was baking a cake for the Holiday when Daniel came downstairs the next morning, his drum hanging from his neck.

"Where are you going?" little Chelise asked.

"Out," he said.

Chelise ran to Mother and proclaimed that Daniel was up to something. But Mother ignored her, and a thankful Daniel slipped out the back door unnoticed.

He pulled his jacket tight around his shoulders and headed for the subway station. The City was gray on this December morning. Fresh snow hadn't fallen for a week, and the piles on sidewalks were dirty. Six days until the big Holiday, when everyone would exchange gifts to celebrate the world's prosperity. The City was in a mad rush to show just how prosperous it really was.

Daniel rode the train in silence, just a boy with a drum, headed nowhere as far as the other passengers were concerned. But he had a mission. A mission that seemed silly and crazy and even dangerous now that he was headed downtown.

He'd memorized the words to the "Little Drummer Boy" song and the rhythm for the *pa—rum—pum—pum—pum* part that he'd heard in his dream. He mumbled the words under his breath as the train rolled toward the City center. They gave him some comfort, but not much. Maybe he really was just a foolish boy with dangerous dreams.

The moment Daniel stepped off the train and

stared at the towering City Hall building, he knew that he was just that. Nothing but a silly boy who should turn right around and head back home.

But he didn't. He lowered his head and climbed the broad steps. The Mayor worked here. Daniel entered City Hall and stopped, unsure where to find him.

"Can I help you, young boy?" a man in a gray uniform asked.

"I'm looking for the Mayor," Daniel said.

"The Mayor, eh? He's in the council meeting. It's a public meeting. No reason you can't go in." He pointed the way. "Up the stairs, down that hall, last door on the right. And I suggest you stay in the balcony. They won't permit any foolishness."

"Thank you, sir," Daniel said. He hugged his drum tight under his arm and headed to the stairs.

For the most part, city council meetings were scary. A hundred men and women dressed in stuffy, dark clothes filled the chairs on the main floor. The Mayor sat behind a long wooden table at the front with six men on either side.

The chairman banged a gavel, and council members shouted. They were doing what all good lawmakers did to determine important things.

Daniel held his drum with both hands and watched it all from the balcony with other City dwellers. News cameras filmed the meeting.

Slowly the hours ticked by, and slowly Daniel became more and more certain that he'd made a mistake in coming. This wasn't the place for a young boy with a drum.

But then he thought about the drum, floating to his bed, calling to him in his dream. *Play for him, Daniel. Go on, play for him.*

He stared at the drum. If only he could really play this drum the way Father could! There was nothing he wanted more.

Daniel tried to bend his wrists, but they were fixed. He ran his hand over the skin of the drum, feeling the texture. And then he whispered quietly so no one could hear him.

"I will play for you. If you are the king and if the Little Drummer Boy once played for you on this drum, then I will play it for you again. I promise I will. And I'll drum for you like no one else, you'll see. You really will. I . . ."

The chairman was banging his gavel. "Then if there are no further petitions for business, we will close the session."

Daniel's heart bolted in his chest. The meeting was over!

"I motion we adjourn this meeting," someone said.

"I second that motion," another said. The room rumbled with talk.

Daniel leapt to his feet without thinking. "Wait!"

The chairman looked up to the balcony. "What was that?"

A hundred people turned Daniel's way. "I . . . I have something," he said.

For a moment no one spoke.

"Is that allowed?" someone asked. "He's a child."

"What is it?" the chairman asked.

"I have a petition," Daniel said, repeating words that he'd heard all day long.

"Well, then move yourself down here so that you don't have to yell," the chairman said. "Hurry now."

Daniel walked timidly down the stairs and then headed up the long aisle, past the chairs toward the front, trying to ignore all the stares. He stopped ten feet from the long table. Only half the members were even looking at him. The Mayor was listening to someone speaking in his ear.

"Speak up, boy," the chairman said.

Daniel cleared his throat, but his voice squeaked when he spoke. "I would like to play my drum for Baby Jesus," he said.

Silence gripped the room. The Mayor now stared directly at Daniel, whose knees began to shake. The television cameras focused on him and whirred loudly.

"What?" the chairman asked.

"I . . . I said that—"

"I know what you said," the man interrupted. "It's against the law."

"Can you change the law?" Daniel asked.

A murmur broke out. The Mayor, a large man with an imposing stare, straightened and gave Daniel a smile that didn't seem friendly.

"Laws exist for a good reason, lad. Reasons you wouldn't understand. Fables that offend people have no place in our City."

"But I don't think it's a fable!" Daniel said. "I know the story of Jesus and how he loved the poor and healed the sick. Why can't I play my drum for him?"

The Mayor blinked. Sweat glistened on his upper lip. "It's a fable, everyone knows it's a fable," the Mayor snapped. "No one believes that absurd little story. There is no such thing as . . ."

He stopped short.

"Christmas?" Daniel said. "That's what they used to call the Holiday. A king came and saved the world, and everyone used to celebrate his birthday on December 25. I'm poor and can't give much of anything, but I think I could play this drum for him. Can I do that?"

The black–suited men stared. The camera whirred. Daniel's heart thumped.

"No," the Mayor said, his face turning red. "Little boys don't understand how things work, but adults do, and we say no. Christmas is a silly fable that only hurt the world."

Then the Mayor snatched the gavel from the chairman's hand and struck the table hard. "This meeting is adjourned."

Daniel stood in the living room with Chelise and his parents, staring at the television. He didn't understand why his small question could cause such big trouble, but Father's scowl told Daniel he was in for it.

"You're like a star," Chelise said, watching the tube with wide eyes.

"How could you do this to me, Daniel?" Father demanded. "You've never disobeyed me like this. Never!"

The television showed Daniel standing in front of the Mayor with his drum. "I'm sorry, Father. You said that I could only play the drum for Jesus if the Mayor changed the law. I only went to ask him."

"Did you really think you could just walk in and change history? There's a reason why Christmas has been unlawful since before you were born." He shook his head. "You're lucky they didn't throw you in prison, boy!"

"Father," his mother said, "Daniel was only trying to honor you by getting permission."

"He's a movie star!" Chelise said. "I want to be on television, too."

"Hush, Chelise," Mother said. She faced Father. "It's just an interesting story, dear. There's no damage."

"I know the City," Father said. "It won't take much to throw these people into a fit."

Daniel felt terrible for making Father so upset.

"Did you ever believe in Christmas, Father?" he asked.

Father hesitated. "No," he said. "Not really, no. The Christmas story is a fable and caused enough trouble, that's for sure."

"So then the king named Jesus never was born?" Daniel cried. "He never healed the man's hand?"

Father's pause was even longer this time. "Where did you hear such a thing?"

"But is it true?"

"Maybe once upon a time it was, Daniel," Mother said. "But it doesn't really matter. We live in a new world now."

"The drum should be burned," Father said.

Daniel snatched his drum off the counter. "Burned? No, please! Please . . ."

"All this Christmas nonsense has caused too much trouble. It's just a drum!"

Daniel's mind whirled.

"If it's just a drum, then it can't cause any real trouble, right? What can a little boy with an old wooden drum do to upset the City?"

They all looked at each other for a few moments. Father frowned.

"He's just a boy," Mother said.

"Can I be on television?" Chelise asked.

"Hush, Chelise," Mother and Father said in unison.

Father stood and took the drum from the sofa. He put it in a cabinet, turned the key to lock it in, and shoved his finger at the locked door. "The drum stays locked up until this nonsense is done."

Then he stormed out of the room.

DANIEL CLIMBED INTO BED feeling very sad that night. Maybe Father was right. Maybe he'd just imagined the drum coming to him. Maybe it was all just a fairy tale.

He pulled the papers out from under his mattress where he'd hidden them and read them again, late into the night, three times, and with each reading he became more convinced that Christmas was real. That a king named Jesus had been born in a town called Bethlehem long ago. That the baby had grown up and done wonderful things that no ordinary man could ever have done.

How could the City pretend such an amazing man never lived?

But none of that mattered now. The drum was locked away. He loved Father and must obey him. The trip to City Hall had been a mistake.

And yet, Daniel couldn't stop feeling sad. He sat on the side of his bed and began to cry. He felt a little foolish, so he locked his door, but he couldn't stop crying as he thought about the forgotten king. How could anyone say that Christmas was hurtful?

He finally stopped crying and fell asleep. And he dreamed.

Play for him, Daniel. Go on, play for him.

It was perhaps the most wonderful dream he'd ever had. If he couldn't actually play for the king, then he would do it in his dream, at the manger with Mary and Baby Jesus smiling. The song seemed so real that he wondered if it might wake up the house.

Daniel woke and sat up with a start. Gray light filtered through the curtain with an early dawn. The house was still except for his own breathing.

And then he saw the drum, sitting on his dresser. There in his room, not in the locked cabinet downstairs.

He caught his breath. A *tick* sounded in the rafters. The drum had come to him again? Unless Father had changed his mind and placed it on his dresser.

Daniel jumped out of bed and ran to the cabinet door. It was still locked! He whirled to the dresser, and stared at the drum in awe. It had come to him!

He picked up the drum and examined it carefully. Still the same drum that he'd played yesterday. But this obviously was no ordinary drum.

He almost ran from the room to show Mother and Father, but immediately thought better of it. Father would only say he'd taken it from the cabinet and lock it up again. He couldn't risk that, because he now knew that he would, he *must*, play this drum for the king.

Daniel returned to his bed, thoughts of wonder spinning in his head, and he lay quiet until he heard his father leave for the Circus an hour later.

Today was December 22. Only three more days until the Holiday. Three more days until Christmas, which was no longer Christmas.

Daniel heard the door slam downstairs. He quickly dressed, scooped up the drum, and slipped out the back before Chelise could corner him.

Once again Daniel took the subway downtown and walked up the steps to the City Hall, hiding his drum as best he could. Once again he found his way to the balcony above the council meeting where the same dark suits from yesterday were arguing the same ways over many important things.

When the meeting neared the end, he slipped down to the main floor and waited at the back.

The chairman said, "So if there aren't any more items of business . . ."

"Excuse me," Daniel said, stepping into the aisle. "I have something." All watched in astonishment as he walked toward the front.

"I think the world should know that Jesus was born in a town called Bethlehem in a manger a long time ago. And I think the City should honor him with a celebration, just like we celebrate George Washington and Martin Luther King, Jr. and Independence Day."

"Hold on, boy," the chairman said, raising his gavel.

"I think Christmas is real," Daniel said. And although he hadn't planned such a daring thing, he began to beat on the drum hanging from his neck.

Pa rum pum pum pum. Pa rum pum pum pum.

The cameras whirred in the background. Otherwise, the council and all those gathered remained perfectly silent.

Pa rum pum pum pum. Pa rum pum pum pum.

Daniel couldn't hold himself back any longer. He began to sing in a small but clear voice.

Come, they told me, pa rum pum pum pum
A newborn King to see, pa rum pum pum pum . . .

They watched him with gaping mouths, too stunned to stop him. So he sang the next verse.

Little Baby, pa rum pum pum pum
I am a poor boy too, pa rum pum pum pum
I have no gift to bring, pa rum pum pum pum . . .

He was so frightened, standing all alone, that he couldn't play the beat well, but his voice gained strength and he sang the words clearly.

"I object!" a council member finally cried. "This is an outrage! The boy should be whipped and thrown in prison!"

"Who let him back in?" another yelled.

And still another, "Does this boy have parents?"

Arguments broke out, and Daniel thought he might be crushed by the loud voices. His knees were shaking so badly that he thought he might have to sit down.

The Mayor took the gavel and banged it. "Silence!"

The room quieted.

"Are you deaf, boy? I told you yesterday, this ridiculous fable does nothing but cause trouble, and your being here today is proof of that. No one is interested in the birth of this Jesus. The Holiday is about prosperity and gifts and food, not some mythological child born over two thousand years ago!"

"Punish him!" the Chairman snapped.

"Do you want to go to prison?" the Mayor asked angrily.

"I . . ." What could he say? "I think that he was born for me, so maybe I should play for him," Daniel said.

"If you do," the Mayor shot back, "then you and your family will be in terrible trouble, young boy. I suggest you leave and never come back."

Snow fell like a heavy blanket as Daniel walked back to his house. The moment he stepped inside, he met Father's stern gaze.

"How dare you break into the cabinet and remove the drum!"

"I didn't! The drum came . . ."

"To your room," Father said. "You'll not have any supper tonight! It's time you learned your lesson."

His mother and Chelise both looked at him with sympathy in their eyes.

Daniel went up to his room with a heavy heart,

sat on his bed, and began to cry. After he ran out of tears, he crossed his legs and sat quietly.

Mother and Father were arguing loudly downstairs about what he'd done, arguing over whether Christmas was real. And it sounded like Father was having second thoughts about being so hard on Daniel.

He could hear people on the television talking as well. The cameras had recorded his singing, and they were playing it over and over. He'd put the City in an uproar.

Daniel woke up the next morning to the sight of Chelise standing in his doorway.

"It's still snowing," she said.

He looked at her without speaking.

"Are you sad?" she asked.

"Yes. I think I am," he said.

"You're like a star. You sang on television."

"I don't feel like a star."

"They all want to know if you're going to do it again," she said, sitting on the end of his bed.

"Do what?"

"Disobey the council and sing the song about Christmas again. Is it true?"

It occurred to Daniel that if everyone had heard the song on television, then thousands, maybe even millions of children just like Chelise were hearing about the king's birth for the first time. How many others were whispering questions about Christmas this morning, just like Chelise?

He sat up and nodded. "Yes! It is true. It has to be true."

"How do you know?"

"Because if it wasn't true, no one would be so upset, would they? And can you keep a secret?"

"Of course."

"The cabinet was locked. The drum came into my room by itself."

She stared at him for a moment. "Tell me more. And tell me about this Jesus."

And so Daniel told Chelise all about the baby who was born to be king. And as he did, he knew that he really was the Drummer Boy, letting all who would dare hear that the king had been born to save this world.

THE SNOW FELL FOR TWO MORE DAYS without letting up, immobilizing the City, stopping the big rush for gifts that normally crowded the streets right before the Holiday.

Daniel woke early on Holiday morning and looked around his bedroom curtain to the street below. It was December 25 and the City was blanketed by a falling white sky. Not a single soul disturbed the thick layer of powder.

A great sadness flooded Daniel. This was the day that the world had once celebrated the coming of the Savior, but today that truth was smothered like the snow smothered the ground.

But beneath the silence, Daniel knew the whole City was talking in whispers, arguing like Mother and Father.

Maybe Daniel really was meant to play the Drummer Boy's drum so that the world would know once again that the Holiday really was about the Baby Jesus.

Maybe Daniel really was the Little Drummer Boy.

He suddenly knew what he would do. What he must do. Daniel slipped on his jacket, picked up his drum, and sneaked out the front door.

The snow was cold and the sky was still gray. He walked out to the middle of the street and looked north, toward City Hall's tall spire.

He hung the drum on his neck and looked around. The street was empty.

"This is for you, my king," he said. And then he

began to pat the drum softly. *Pa rum pum pum pum.*

His arms were stiff and he didn't strike the beat perfectly every time, but that didn't matter. No one was listening anyway. No one except the king, who smiled like he did the last time the drum had been played for him.

Pa rum pum pum pum. Daniel beat the drum with a little more force, gaining confidence. And then he began to sing:

> *Come, they told me, pa rum pum pum pum*
> *A newborn King to see, pa rum pum pum pum*
> *Our finest gifts we bring, pa rum pum pum pum*
> *To lay before the King, pa rum pum pum pum,*
> *rum pum pum pum, rum pum pum pum,*
> *So to honor Him, pa rum pum pum pum,*
> *When we come.*

"Shut up, boy!" a voice cried from the next building.

Daniel looked at the man who was leaning out of the window.

"That's divisive, don't you know?"

Daniel wanted to play more, he really did. What if the man did something nasty?

But Daniel couldn't help himself. He played anyway, beating the drum gently.

"Are you deaf, boy?"

"He's playing for the king!" a shrill voice called to his right. Chelise stood on the front steps, holding an old toy drum that Father had given her two years earlier. She held the old man's gaze for a moment.

"He has to play," she said, and then she started to beat her drum.

Daniel began to sing again as they played together.

Little Baby, pa rum pum pum pum
I am a poor boy too, pa rum pum pum pum
I have no gift to bring, pa rum pum pum pum
That's fit to give a King, pa rum pum pum pum,
rum pum pum pum, rum pum pum pum,

Shall I play for You, pa rum pum pum pum,
On my drum?

"If you don't stop this foolishness this minute," the neighbor called, red-faced, "I swear I'll . . ."

"You'll go back into your house, Graham," a familiar voice boomed.

Daniel twisted back to the corner of their house. Father stood in the snow. A large tom-tom drum hung from his neck. Beside him stood Mother holding a plastic bucket.

And then Father began to beat on the drum, taking up the same beat with the confidence of a master drummer. Three drums now, beating in unison. Mother beat on her bucket.

Daniel smiled wide and hit his drum harder. *Pa rum pum pum pum.* And he sang in a clear voice that rang down the street now.

Mary nodded, pa rum pum pum pum

The ox and lamb kept time, pa rum pum pum pum
I played my drum for Him, pa rum pum pum pum
I played my best for Him, pa rum pum pum pum,
rum pum pum pum, rum pum pum pum,
Then He smiled at me, pa rum pum pum pum,
Me and my drum.

Then he started all over again, playing his drum for the whole world to hear. A window slid open down the street. Daniel could hear the drum being beaten before he saw it, just inside. Four drums and a plastic bucket now, in unison.

Another window slid open and Mary Summers leaned out, beating the rhythm on her window sill. Down the street Jerry Roth flipped a garbage can over and started to beat on his makeshift drum like a champ.

Two doors opened, then a third. The street came alive with rhythmic beating. Some had drums, others used pots, others garbage cans, and still others struck windows and walls.

Grinning wide in giddy delight, Daniel stood in the middle of the street leading the orchestra in this announcement of the Christ child's birth. He began to sing clear and strong for them all to hear, *"Come, they told me, Pa rum pum pum pum; A newborn King to see, Pa rum pum pum pum."*

And then an amazing thing happened. Someone on the adjacent street joined in. The City had been debating this song for three days now, and it seemed that the call to join had somehow become irresistible.

Daniel could see them more than hear them—dozens, maybe hundreds of people beating out the cadence. *Pa rum pum pum pum.*

He sang the song again, hardly able to contain himself. For a moment, and only a moment, he stopped playing. What greeted his ears nearly took his breath away. A dull thunder rose from the skyline in almost perfect unison:

Pa rum pum pum pum. Pa rum pum pum pum.

Hundreds, thousands, maybe a hundred thousand, maybe the whole City, pounding out a welcome for the king loud enough to wake the dead!

And they had, Daniel thought. They had awakened Christmas from the dead.

Daniel threw his head back, beat on his drum, and began to sing again at the top of his lungs.

"Come, they told me, pa rum pum pum pum; A newborn King to see, pa rum pum pum pum!"

For the first time in many, many years, the old remembered why they had once paid homage to this king called Jesus. And for the first time, countless children learned that there was a king deserving of such a thundering welcome on Christmas morning.

The Little Drummer Boy had indeed played once more for Christ the king, but, more importantly, the king himself had come again, illuminating their minds and hearts in a time of total darkness.

THE END

More from the Mind of Ted Dekker...

If *The Drummer Boy* touched your heart, you'll also love *The Promise,* Ted Dekker's Christmas tale about a mute boy who clings to the hope that one day a King will give him a voice.

With more than a million novels sold and several number one bestsellers, Ted Dekker is known for mind–bending, adrenaline–laced thrillers, including:

Showdown

A black-cloaked man arrives at the sleepy town of Paradise with the power to grant any unfulfilled dream. He is irresistible. Seems like bliss…but is it? Or is all hell about to break loose in Paradise?

Obsessed

As a man frantically pursues his family's lost legacy, someone pursues him—someone equally obsessed with the prize. Looks like the man most obsessed will gain everything. And the loser will lose all.

House
With coauthor Frank Peretti

In a killer's game, the only way to win is to lose and the only way out is in. One game, seven players, three rules.

Visit TedDekker.com to discover more.